Contents

To the teacher

This series of three books is intended to help pupils with practice material at that rudimentary level which has previously been neglected by published materials. It doesn't keep pupils busy with meaningless tasks, but gets them started on essential practice in what they will need in later life.

The language level is deliberately simple and direct. The books tell pupils why they need to bother with rules and presentation, i.e. for the sake of their audience.

The books offer the essentials only; the frills can be found elsewhere. The layout presents one topic per page or double page, which probably corresponds to one lesson per item.

These topics are deliberately self-contained so that they can be either followed in sequence or dipped into for special practice. The whole range of writing, reading, speaking, listening and imaginative work is covered, and cross-referenced in the index on page 48, so that skills can be practised either in linear sequence or in rotation.

The whole point of the series is to tell the pupils why they are doing something; to set them a clear task; to get them to check for themselves; then for you to mark their work. In this way problems in spelling or understanding can be diagnosed early, and further practice work supplied if necessary.

All teaching preparation is contained in the book. The only time you have to go outside it is for an atlas on page 12. Don't worry if you're covering for someone else's lesson; the book will give you everything you need!

CP 2
R1
17.78

PRACTICAL ENGLISH 2

Kenneth Ireland

Macmillan Education

Acknowledgement

The two instructions on page 11 are reproduced courtesy of Curry's.

First published 1986

Published by
MACMILLAN EDUCATION LTD
Houndmills, Basingstoke, Hampshire RG21 2XS
and London
Companies and representatives
throughout the world

Designed by Sue Williams
Illustrated by Maggie Ling

Filmsetting by Vantage Photosetting Co. Ltd
Eastleigh and London
Printed in Hong Kong

British Library Cataloguing in Publication Data
Ireland, Kenneth
Practical English.
2
1. English language—Grammar—1950
I. Title
428 PE1112

ISBN 0–333–40545–5

Before you start

This book doesn't bother with things which you don't need, but only with things which you do need. There is nothing provided in it just to give you something to do, but everything will teach you something that you either might have forgotten or didn't know in the first place.

If you can read what I've written so far, then you can read anything in this book. If you found it hard to read so far, then you'll be much better before long.

The whole book makes sure that you get the hang of things, giving you starting points or reasons for doing things. All you have to do is to read and make sense of what you are reading, to write so that others can see at once what you mean, to talk so that others can tell what you're talking about – straight away – and to be able to listen and understand what others are saying.

It's easy, so don't think that it isn't.

Two things – where you see the word **check**, it means *stop and take a good look at what you've done*. Read it and check it carefully. No written work is finished until you have read it through carefully. When it says **have it marked** – well, that makes sense, doesn't it? And making sense is where we'll start.

1 *Making sense*

i whent to th pichers on satday and it was grate we got their early and sor this flim it was about a man how could fli.

If you write something, it's because you want somebody to read it – easily. So it's got to make sense. If it doesn't, you've wasted everybody's time, including your own.

1 How many sentences should there be in that *horrible example* at the top of the page?

Where should you put capital letters?

Which words have been spelt wrong? And which words have been spelt wrong because the letters have been mixed up?

2 **Write** it as it should have been done. I've found 15 mistakes to put right, counting the missing capital letters and full stops.

When you've done it, **check**.

Yours should be *perfect*, no mistakes at all. Is it? If so, **have it marked**.

3 Now – do better. If this is the start of the year at school, or the start of a new term, you must have done *something* during the holiday you've just had. Don't write about all of the holiday, and don't start thinking that you didn't do anything – you did! You must have got out of bed sometime.

Pick just one or two interesting things which you did, that's all. Or if you did one really great thing, pick that.

Put the title:

Best parts of the holiday

and **write** about them. Ask the teacher for any spellings you need.

Break your writing up into *paragraphs*, if you can manage it. Your teacher will tell you how to do this, but a paragraph contains one topic. When you move on to something a little different, you start a new paragraph.

When you've finished, **check**. Read it through slowly. Does it make sense to you? If it does, most likely it will to anyone else. If something's wrong, cross it out neatly and put it right.

Then **have it marked**.

2 *Talking*

Talking has to make sense, too. In fact, talking is often more important than writing, because you talk a lot more than you write, even in school.

1 Some of the class can talk about what they did in the holidays, if they can't think of a better idea yet. As long as it was interesting to them, then it will be interesting to most other people. Or, if it's not near a holiday, what they did at the weekend, or the night before.

They can talk for as long as they like providing they don't go on for so long that it becomes boring. Any of the rest of the class can ask a question, as long as it's sensible.

2 What people do can be interesting. Somebody might have a hobby, or a pet to look after, or something like that. If anyone collects things, he or she could take some of them to school and show the rest of the class as well, while talking about them. If it's something you don't do yourself, then *listen* and learn something. If there's something which *you* do, it's what helps to make you interesting, so you might as well talk about it.

3 You ought to know what's going on in the world, which you can find from TV, or the radio, or the newspapers – anywhere. Every now and then it's a good idea if the teacher mentions something that's been in the news, and asks if anyone knows anything about it. Somebody will. It might as well be you. You try to find out what's going on all the time, so you can take part. See if you notice any *odd* items of news – like the policemen who were telling somebody that they'd found his stolen bike, and while they were telling him somebody else stole it again from outside the police station.

4 You could try a game of *Twenty Questions*. If you have used Book One then you'll know how to play it. It helps to make you think logically. In case you didn't use Book One, here it is again.

Everything can be divided into *animal*, *vegetable* or *mineral*. *Animal* means any kind of creature which has lived, or anything made from it, or part of it. *Vegetable* means anything that's grown in the ground, or anything made from vegetables, or part of a vegetable. *Mineral* is everything else found in the air or in the ground, or made from that thing.

Four people leave the room and don't cheat (and neither do their friends, by trying to tell them when they come back). While they are out, the teacher writes an object on the blackboard so that everyone can read it (but *not* aloud). Then the teacher rubs it off, and the four outside come back in. Somebody keeps the score. The four have not more than twenty questions to find out what was written on the blackboard, and usually the only answers allowed are either *yes* or *no*. The only clue given is whether the object is animal, vegetable or mineral.

It's easy, and interesting, once you have played the first game and got the idea . . . which is not to guess, but to work it out.

3 *How to use it*

You'd be surprised how many people can't tell others how to use their record player, television or video. The reason is that they don't think out what *the other person really needs to know*.

Some people don't know the names of things, either, like the difference betwen a switch, a knob, a lever, a catch or a handle. They just use the word *thing*: 'There's a thing that you turn . . .'

What is the difference between a switch, a knob and a lever?
What is the difference between a catch and a handle?

1 Now – you've probably got a TV set. *How do you use it?* Your television set is most likely not quite the same as everybody else's. Where do you plug it in? How do you switch it on or off? Where are the controls for volume, brightness, contrast, colour perhaps – and do you turn them, slide them, or what? How do you change channels?

So, **write** down how to use your television set. You might need to draw a little plan showing where everything is, to help.

2 Think of something else which you have. It might be a record player, a video recorder or game, an electric lawnmower, a sewing machine, a camera, a digital watch – or anything like that. *How do you make it work?* If it's a digital watch, you could explain how to set the time, the date and the seconds.

Check. Could anyone read your instructions and follow them?
If so, **have it marked**.

Read these two sets of instructions. Are they simple enough to understand?

HOW TO USE YOUR TOASTER

1. COLOUR SELECTOR LEVER
This lever selects the brownness of toast . . . start at the middle of toast range and move lighter or darker to suit your desire for toast colour.

2. TOASTING
Insert bread into wells. NOTE: When toasting a single slice of bread, you must always use the well marked "one slice". Push down on knob to lower bread to the latched position; this starts toasting cycle. Toast will pop up AUTOMATICALLY when selected colour has been reached. To stop toasting before automatic pop-up, simply lift up on the knob.

Reheat Cold Toast
Just toast as usual. Toast pops up again quickly, piping hot – with little – if any – colour change.

OPERATING INSTRUCTIONS
Currys Dry Iron - Models BL86/88

Operation
1. Temperature setting
The markings on the heat selector dial are those recommended by the Home Laundry Consultative Committee (H.L.C.C.) which aims, with the co-operation of textile, appliance and detergent manufacturers, to standardise the marking of their products so that washing and ironing is made easier for the housewife.
The settings and a guide to the fabrics for which they are suitable, are as follows:

●●●	HOT	Cotton, linen, rayon and modified rayon
●●	WARM	Polyester mixtures, wool
●	COOL	Acrylic nylon acetate, tri-acetate, polyester, silk

If in any doubt always start with the lower temperature setting.

2. Before Ironing
Sort the clothing into groups and start with materials which need the coolest setting, gradually working up the scale.

3. Plug in the Iron
The neon indicator will now light up.

4. Ready for use
When the iron reaches the temperature selected on the dial, the neon indicator will go out. The indicator will continue to light up and go out as ironing proceeds, indicating that the iron is maintaining the selected temperature.

5. Changing to another temperature setting
Set the dial to the required position. Your iron is ready for use again when the indicator light goes out (if changing to a higher temperature), or when the indicator light comes on again (if changing to a lower temperature).

6. When not in use
The iron may be stood on its heel.

CAUTION: DO NOT LEAVE WITHOUT SUPERVISION WHEN CONNECTED TO THE MAINS. DO NOT WRAP THE CORD AROUND THE IRON WHILST STILL HOT.

4 *Atlas*

This is about reading. But it's also about *doing* something with your reading.

1 You need an atlas (borrowed from the Geography department), and a blank map of the world.

You could trace the outline on this page onto a sheet of paper to paste into your exercise book. If you don't know how to trace, your teacher will be able to show you.

2 In the atlas, find the full map of the world.

On your blank map, mark in these countries:

(a) The country where you live
(b) Mexico
(c) Argentina
(d) Chile
(e) India
(f) Pakistan
(g) Bangladesh
(h) Italy
(i) Spain
(j) Portugal
(k) Finland
(l) The Sudan
(m) Poland
(n) Turkey
(o) Liberia
(p) Korea

And mark in these islands:

(q) Iceland
(r) Sri Lanka
(s) Cuba
(t) Taiwan

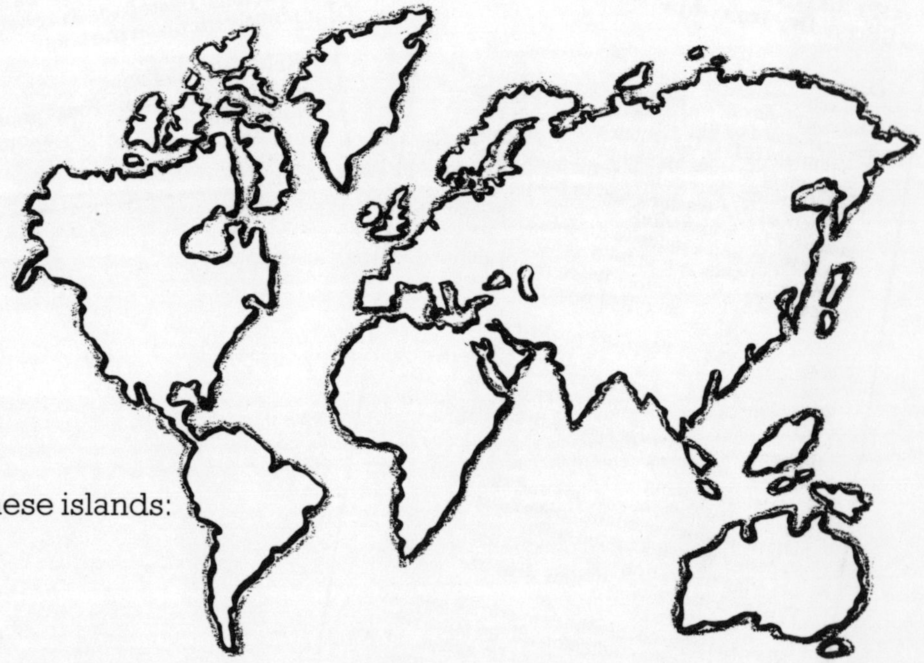

Check. Is your map marked clearly and neatly, so anyone can read it?
Capital letters for names of places?
If so, **have it marked.**

3 Do the same using an atlas and a blank map of your own country. This time, mark in *six main towns* and *two rivers*.

Check.
Have it marked.

5 *Clothes*

Suppose you could wear just whatever you liked, what would you put on? Think – just one set of clothes won't be right for everything.

What would you wear for school? Would you have something different in the summer from what you wore in the winter? What sort of shoes would you wear – remember they have to be fairly sensible ones for school.

What would you wear for just messing about – what you might call *casual* wear? Would those clothes be different in winter?

And if you were going somewhere special, like to a party or something like that, what would you wear then?

1 **Discuss** a few ideas. Suggest a few things. The teacher can write some of the words on the blackboard so that you will be sure to spell them right, if you use them.

2 Give it a title: Clothes I'd like to wear

then **write** what you would wear, and why – for school (summer and winter), for messing about, for going somewhere when you have to look nice. Never mind what's in fashion – you decide what *you* would like. (And don't decide to become a nudist and wear nothing at all! That would be too easy.) If it helps, draw pictures as well. Write a paragraph for each of the three lots of clothing.

Check. Sentences? Easy to read? Does it all make sense?
If so, **have it marked**.

6 *Letters*

Do you remember how to set out a letter – properly?

You start *not with your name* but your address, beginning about the *middle* of the top line, to leave space for the rest of the address. A capital letter to start each word, remember!

Write the date underneath the address.

Over on the left, you start with *Dear* and whatever the name is, on the same line, ending with a comma.

Start the letter itself with a capital somewhere under the name you've just written.

To finish off, you write whatever words suit the person you're writing to.

Sign it with whatever you are called.

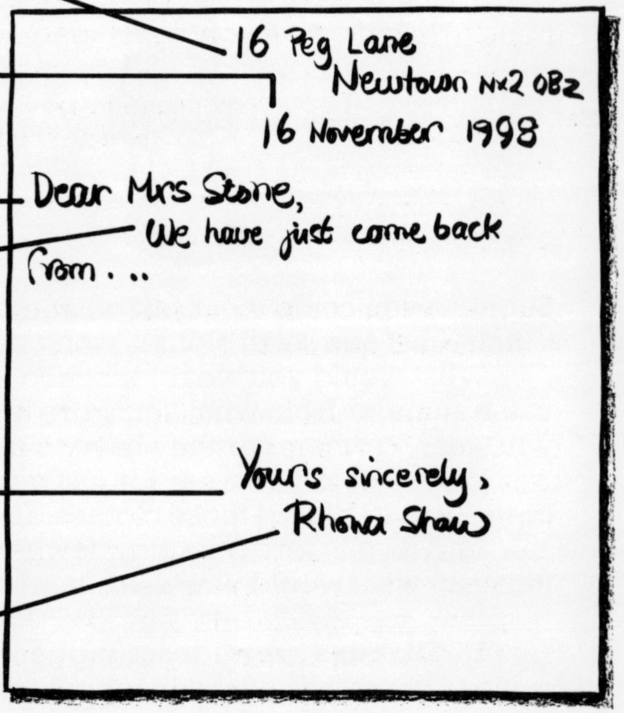

1 You've just spent a weekend at the home of a friend or relation. When you get home, you find you've left something behind by mistake. Your friend or relation isn't on the telephone, so you must write a letter, and it's too far away for you to go back easily.

What should go in the letter? How should you start it? What do you want them to do with what you've left behind? They can either keep it till you go again, or they can bring it with them when they come to see you, or they can post it to you. If you want them to post it, you'll need to say that you'll give them the money if they let you know how much it cost. *You* have to decide what you want them to do.

How should you finish off the letter before you write *Yours sincerely*? **Write** the letter.

Check. Set out properly? Makes complete sense?
If so, **have it marked**.

2 One of the hardest letters to write is to thank a relative for a present, because it's always hard to think what to put – especially if the one who has sent you the present doesn't see you very often, so you don't know him or her very well. What you have to do is thank the person for the present, say how you liked it or what you've done with it, add a bit of news perhaps – then find some way of finishing it off.

Now, suppose an old aunt, who hasn't seen you since you were a baby, can't remember how old you are and has sent you something for your birthday which is *no use to you at all,* like a little teddy bear or something. You mustn't upset your very old aunt, because she didn't know any better, but you must write and thank her.

Write the letter. Her name is Aunt Hilda – or Aunty Hilda, if that's what she likes to be called.

Check. Can you read all of it? Is it nice and friendly and polite?
If so, **have it marked**.

7 *Acting*

You need space in front of the classroom. Move the front row well back, perhaps, so there's plenty of room to move about properly.

For those who want to join in with the plays I'm going to suggest, get into groups of the right number, then work out how each play is going to be done, who's going to do what in it, and so on. If two or three groups are going to try the same play, the play ought to get better each time as one group learns from any mistakes of those who acted it before them.

Do not have more than about three groups doing the same play, though, or you'll find the same things being done too often.

While each play is being performed, the rest of the class are the *audience* - and watching.

1 A *mime* is where nobody says a word, and it's all done in silence. This is a very good mime for two people.

The two are walking along a street. It's a Saturday, and they're bored. Perhaps they are kicking odd pebbles about. Then one notices a coin in the gutter and picks it up. They take it along with them to a sweet shop window, but can't decide what to spend the money on. So at last they toss for it to decide. They lose the coin, look for it , can't find it anywhere, and at last go off walking along the street, still bored.

The actors are to say nothing, and to use nothing but the space in front of the class, but the rest of the class must be able to know *from their acting* that they are bored, there's nothing to do, that it is a coin which they find, that there is a shop window and that they can't make up their minds . . . etc.

The next few ideas are not mimes. People need to speak, and say what they think would be said.

2 Two chairs are needed, side by side, to be the space outside the Head Teacher's room. One of the class turns up to see the Head Teacher. It might be that this one knows what for – something he or she has done wrong, perhaps – or it might be that this one has no idea why he or she has to see the Head. While that one is there, another of the school, either from the same class or a different class, turns up as well.

What happens now? End it how you like, but do give it a good ending.

3 For this you need a boy and a girl. The girl is waiting at a bus stop, at night, by herself. (What would she be doing? Would she be scared, bored, or what?) Then along comes a boy she knows who tries to chat her up.

What happens – does she tell him where to get off, or clobber him, or what?

Another way to do this is to have a boy turn up whom she *doesn't* know, and see what happens then.

Another way is for a boy to be waiting by himself at the bus stop and a girl tries to pick him up.

Give the play an ending.

4 Somebody arrives late in class. Use the classroom as it is, with somebody acting as the teacher and the rest in their usual places. Then the last one comes in. (How – in a hurry, cross, or what?) The teacher tells him or her off, perhaps. So what's the excuse, and what happens then?

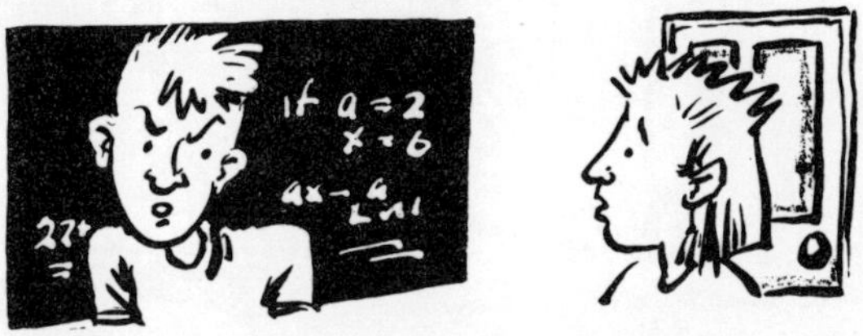

5 *Stuck in a lift.* Use about four people, all taking different parts. Perhaps a woman who's been shopping, an old man, a couple of naughty boys or girls – or whatever you like. The lift stops, suddenly, when it shouldn't have done . . .

6 *The Hi-Jacker* (could be hi-jacking a plane, a bus, or anything). A number can take part, but not too many or it gets mixed up and just ends as a free-for-all. So who is hi-jacking, why are they hi-jacking, how do they set about it, is there any rescue, and who wins in the end?

7 Another play with a fairly large number in it: *Danger at the zoo*. You'll have to think hard about this one. And you'll need some to act as animals. Work it out how you like.

8 Take this title: *Rat poison*. Work out what you can from there!

9 *The last two minutes in bed before going to sleep:* a mime with just one person in it – or two at the very most. It lasts for exactly two minutes. You need two or three desks put together to act as a bed.

10 You've got home at half-past eleven at night, when you should have been home by nine. At least your father or mother is waiting up for you, and nobody is very pleased about it.

Start the play *before* you come in. What's going on, now that you're so late? What are they talking about? Then you come in. Carry on till it comes to a likely end.

11 You could try to **write** a script, perhaps for number 9. Don't have many scenes – two at the most. If possible, just have the one scene, inside the house.

When you write it, you print the names of the characters, then just write what they say. You must start a fresh line each time a character stops talking. Anything you want a character to do, you put inside brackets. These are the *stage directions*. Like:

BOY Oh. (Comes closer.) What is it? (Picks it up and looks at it.)
GIRL It's mine. (Snatches it off him.)

If one or two are any good, they might be acted, but if so the teacher will have to run off enough copies.

Or – **write** it as a radio play and then record it on a cassette recorder. If you do this, you must remember that on radio nobody can *see* what's going on, but only *hear* it. A good test for a radio play, if you think it's any good, is to have it played to another class. They'll soon let you know what they think of it!

8 *Friends*

Choose one of your friends. Now what is this friend like? That is, not only what he or she looks like, but what he or she is *really* like. What's good about him (or her)? Does he do anything special? Is there anything which is not so good, or which you think he should stop doing? What sort of things do you do together?

In fact, work out some details of this person's *character*, what he or she is really like as a person. Is he or she generous, or mean? Smart, or scruffy? Clever, or a bit dumb? . . . that sort of thing. Give examples to show what you mean.

Give it a title. It needn't be the person's name, if you don't want it to be.

Then try to **write** two paragraphs, or perhaps three – who it is, how long you've known him or her, how you first met, what he or she looks like (don't go into too much detail about that). Then – what's good about him or her, what he does well or badly, what he is really like. Finally – something you've done together, or places you go, that sort of thing.

Remember to start the *first* line of each paragraph in from the margin. Ask if you want to know how to spell any words.

When you've finished –
Check. Read it through carefully.
Have it marked.

9 *Your family*

You might belong to a very big family – so big, perhaps, that you don't know much about some of them. Or it might be quite a small one.

1 So what can you say about those you know well? How about who they are? (If you make a list, don't forget to use commas.) Then what's special about each of them? You might have a big brother who's always hitting you, or a little sister who's a pest, or an uncle who spoils you . . . or almost anything. Say what they do, what they are like, and so on.

Give it a title:

My Family

Write about your family. You could write one paragraph about each of them, or if there are rather a lot put several of them into one paragraph. If you are living with one parent, or with people who are not your real family, then write about those you know.

Check. Did you ask for names you weren't sure how to spell? Written neatly? Does it make sense?
If so, **have it marked**.

2 A *Family Tree* can be interesting to work out. Start by working yours out only as far back as your grandparents – even if some of them have died, you can put them in if you know who they were. It would be something like this:

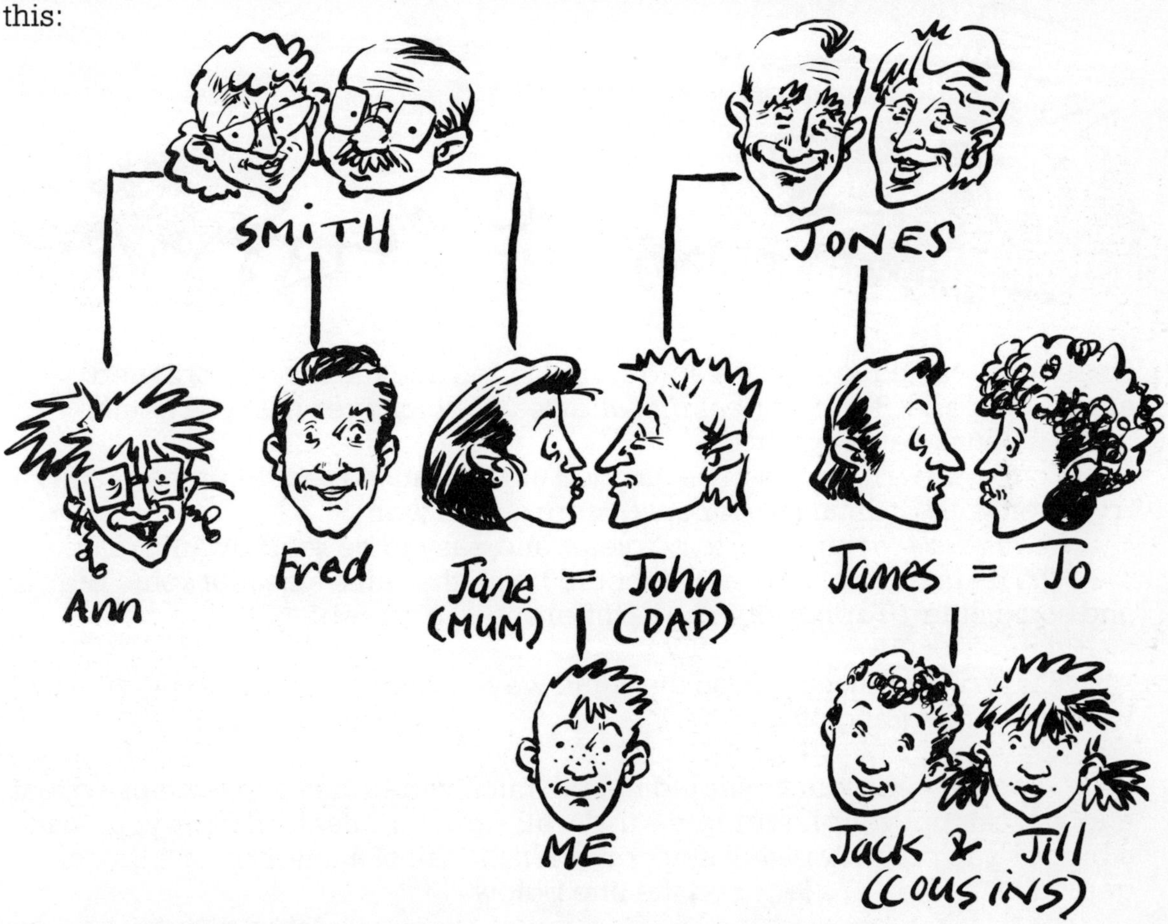

See the idea? What does the equals sign (=) mean?

Now, draw your own family tree, what you know of it. Perhaps you ought to turn your book sideways, and use a clean page.

Start *top left* and *top right* with your two sets of grandparents. Then mark in their children underneath. Make sure that your mother and father finish up next to each other.

Then underneath them, put yourself and any brothers and sisters. Add any of the children of your aunts and uncles which you can fit in – your cousins.

Then add the children of any of your older brothers and sisters, if there are any – these are your nephews and nieces.

Don't put in so many people that it becomes a mess.

Check. Is it neat enough to be able to follow clearly? Capital letters for people's names?
If so, **have it marked**.

10 *Handwriting*

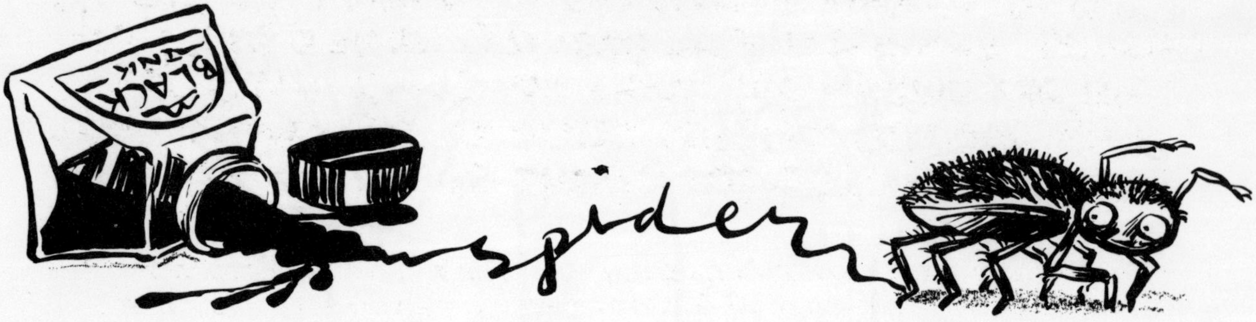

Does your writing look as if a spider had fallen into the ink and crawled across the paper? Or is it *beautiful and neat*? Whichever it is, you could make it better yet, if you tried.

Your *best* writing has to be as good as you can make it when you really try. Then your ordinary writing will improve as well.

Reminder – writing has to be clear, and easy to be read by anybody.

The main parts of the letters should be all the same size, not some big and some little. (Capital letters are different, of course.)

The writing must all slope the same way, not some letters going off one way and some going off another.

Gaps between words should not be much wider than a letter, not a great gap you can put your finger into – that's all right for infants, not for you. Make a bigger gap only after a full stop, or when the tail of a letter on one line is getting in the way of a letter on the line below.

1 Write out the letters of the alphabet, first in small and then in capitals. Don't join the letters up.

abcdefghijklm nopqrst uvwxyz
ABCDEFGH IJKLMNOPQ RSTUVWXYZ

2 Copy in your best writing the paragraph above which begins *Gaps between words . . .*

3 When you've finished, *turn your work upside down* and look at it that way. If it looks neat when it's upside down, then it's most likely all right. Then turn it the right way up and read it through. Made any mistakes?

Gaps between words should not be much wider than a letter, not a great gap you can put your finger into — that's all right for infants not for you. Make a bigger gap only after a full stop, or when the tail of a letter on one line is getting in the way of a letter on the line below.

4 Swap your book with somebody else. **Mark** the other person's writing. Give it a mark out of 10. 8 or 9 upwards would be *very* good, 6 or 7 about average, 5 not all that good, and 3 or 4 (or worse) must be pretty poor. Be honest about the marking. Don't give somebody a good mark just because he or she is a friend, or a low mark because you don't like that other person.

5 When it's all finished, pass the books in and **have them marked** by the teacher, to see if he or she agrees.

It's a good idea for a handwriting exercise to take place at least a couple of times a year, so you don't forget how to write well.

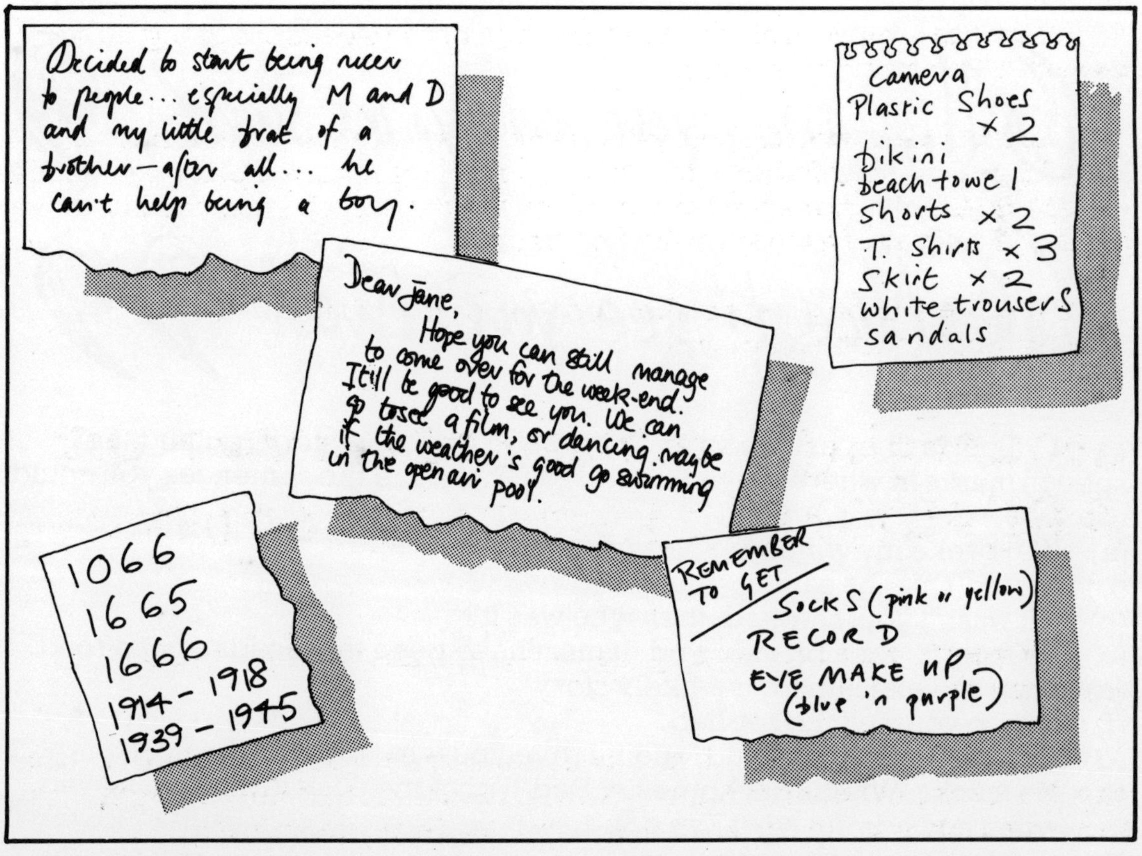

11 *Speech marks*

Speech marks are also called *quotation marks*, or *inverted commas*. Little children are sometimes taught to call them 'sixty-six and ninety-nine'. They are just little marks put at the beginning and end of whenever you quote what somebody says, to make the meaning clear.

You always start speech with a capital letter, and mark off the rest of a sentence with a comma. Like this:

'Hello,' he said.

Or you can use double marks:

"Hello," he said.

Either will do.

Notice – speech marks, capital letter . . . comma, speech marks.

Or the other way round:

He said, 'Hello.' (Notice – comma, speech marks . . .)

If a question is being asked, use a question mark instead of a comma. Like this:

'Where are we going?' he asked.

Where do the speech marks go in this:

Well, he said, what shall we do next?

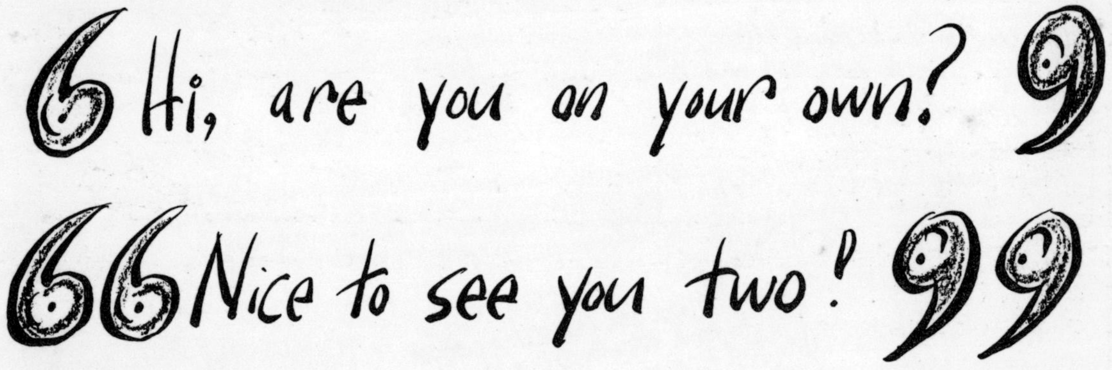

1 Look at the cartoon strip. Then write it out as a story, putting the speech marks in where they are needed. These are the sentences you could use:

(a) You broke my window, she said.
(b) It wasn't me, he said.
(c) If it wasn't you, she said, then who was it?
(d) He thought for a bit then said, It must have been those kids up the road.
(e) That, she exclaimed, is a likely story!
(f) Please yourself, he replied.
(g) You come here, she said, and I'll give you what for.
(h) No thanks. When I get home my Dad'll give me what for, he answered, when he finds out what I've done.

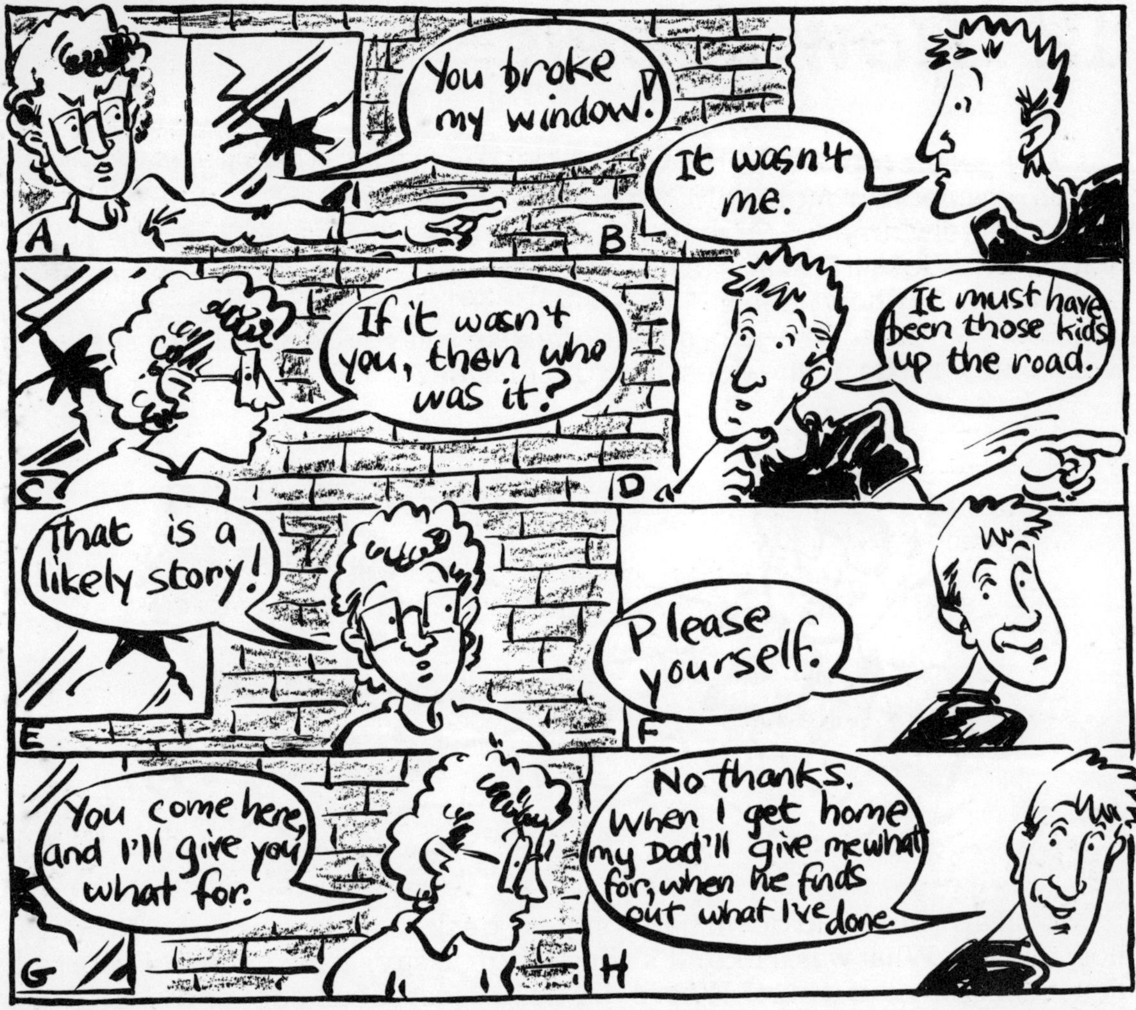

Check. Everything right? Capital letters as well – and the apostrophes? (The what?)
If so, **have it marked**.

2 The other time you use speech marks is round titles of books, TV programmes, or films. (In a newspaper, they use *italics* instead.) Also, you use speech marks to pick out one word in a sentence. When you write a title, you don't use a comma to separate the rest of the sentence.

Put speech marks where they are needed:

(**a**) The Invisible Man was written by H. G. Wells.
(**b**) Enid Blyton wrote the Famous Five books.
(**c**) Did you see the film Raiders of the Lost Ark?
(**d**) Is Nationwide on BBC television after the news?
(**e**) He wasn't sure how to spell description.

Check.
Have it marked.

12 *How it feels*

1 Feel the top of your desk or table. How does it *feel*? Think of the right words . . . smooth, rough, cold, warm, sticky . . . or what?

Now feel your hair. Or even somebody else's. If you can't find the right words, what does it feel *like* instead? It might feel like grass, or a hedgehog, or anything. Say how it feels.

Feel your face. Or again, somebody else's, if you're sure he or she won't bite. Or if he or she does, how did that feel?

2 Slap your hand down hard on your desk or table, just once. Now say how that felt. What was it like? It's not enough to say, 'It hurt.' It didn't hurt all that much! *How* did it hurt? *Where* did it hurt: just in one spot or did it spread, and how long did the feeling last?

Give yourself a good pinch on your arm or leg. Can you say how that felt, in the same way?

3 Take your little fingers and put them both into your mouth so that your top teeth are right on top of the nails. Then *bite hard*, and keep the pressure on for at least half a minute. Then straight away afterwards, hook the ends of your little fingers together, and keeping your little fingers hooked firmly, at once *pull hard*!

Write what it felt like.

Check. Have you described as accurately as you can how it felt?

Some of the class could read out what they have written, to see if the rest of the class had the same experience.

4 At the doctor's or the dentist's or at a hospital, almost every time and for most people it never hurts. But there is always the feeling that it might, isn't there?

Think of some time you went to see a doctor, or a dentist, or if you've been in hospital or visited someone there. This time it might not be a physical feeling which you remember, but a feeling which you had inside you.

Why did you go, what happened to you, and how did it all turn out? And what kinds of feelings did you have while you were there?

Give it a title:

Visit to . . . (whichever it was)

then **write** about it. Ask for any spellings, of course. Write in paragraphs if you can.

Check. You know by now what you are checking for.
Have it marked.

13 *Cars*

How good are you at understanding information?

1 Read this. It's about number plates used on vehicles in Britain:

Until 1963, number plates contained some letters followed by a number, like *EEL 650*. Then in 1963 the number plates had a letter *A* put at the end, like *EEL 650A*. In 1983, the letter reached *Y*. The letter starts to be used in the August of the year before, so actually *Y* started in August, 1982.

It runs like this:
A: 1963, *B*: 1964, *C*: 1965, . . . *S*: 1978, . . . *W*: 1981, *Y*: 1983. If there's a letter at the *front* of the number: *A*: 1984, *B*: 1985, *C*: 1986, and so on.

Letter *I* was not used, because it might look like a number *1*. Letter *Q* was not used, because it might look like an *O*, and *O* was not used because it looked like a number instead of a letter. Letters *U* and *Z* were not used, either.

2 Write the answers to these, in *sentences*:

(a) What year does an *F* mean at the end of a number plate?
(b) What letter was used during 1974?
(c) When was the earliest *month and year* that a car with a number plate *A814 RUY* could have been on the road?
(d) How old is a car with a *V* at the end of its number plate?
(e) What letter was used instead of a *Q*, and what year was that?

3 In Britain, a car number plate also tells *where* the car was first used. The *second two* letters tell you.

For Birmingham, the letters used are:
DA, OA, OB, OC, OF, OG, OH, OJ, OK, OL, OM, ON, OP, OV, OX, UK, VP.

For Nottingham, the letters used are:
AL, AU, NN, NU, RA, RB, RC, TO, TV, VO.

Some others are:
Salisbury: *AA, CG.* Stoke-on-Trent: *BF, FA, RE, RF.* Inverness: *AS.* Bolton: *BN, CB, DK, TD, TE.*

(**a**) Out of Birmingham, Nottingham, Salisbury, Stoke-on-Trent, Inverness and Bolton, which do you think has the biggest number of cars, lorries, buses and motor bikes?
(**b**) Out of those places, which do you think has the smallest number? Why do you think there are so few?

4 Look at these car numbers:

(**a**) Which of these cars were on the road before 1963?
(**b**) Where did these cars come from?
(**c**) Say, for each of the other numbers, where the car came from, *and* the first full year in which it was on the road.

14 *Joining up sentences*

When you write, could you sometimes say the same thing in fewer words if only you thought first? Look at this:

The man stood at the door. The door was open.

You could make that shorter by putting:

The man stood at the door which was open.

Even better, you could write instead:

The man stood at the open door.

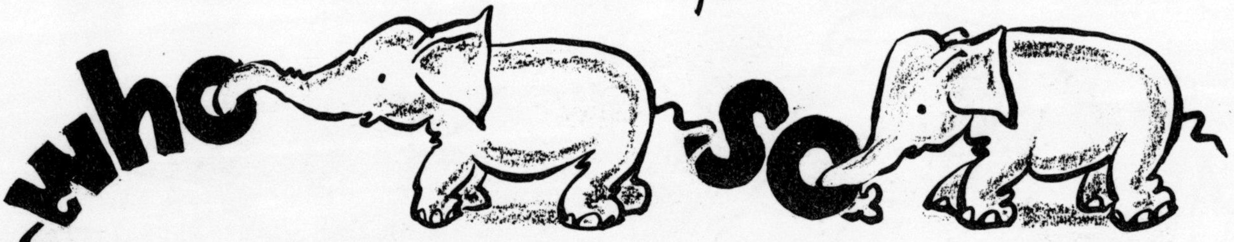

Join these sentences together. *Do not* use *and*, *but* or *so*. (Note – if you use *who*, *which* or *that* for joining, always use *who* for people.)

(**a**) That's the man. He stole my bike.
(**b**) The girl was riding a horse. It looked tired
(**c**) He opened the cupboard. All the books fell out.
(**d**) I saw them in the park. It was five o'clock.
(**e**) The old man climbed the hill. The hill was steep
(**f**) Susan reads badly. She can't see very well.
(**g**) The boy hurt his foot. He limps now.
(**h**) I stayed with my uncle. He lives in the country.
(**i**) This is the house. Jack built the house.

Check. Capital letters and full stops?
Have it marked.

15 *Out of school*

What do you do when you're not at school? Does it depend on the time of the year, and on the weather?

Perhaps you have a hobby of some sort, or somewhere you go, or a club which you visit. Perhaps you just mess about or play with friends somewhere.

Write about the sort of things you do when you're not at school. What do you like doing best, and exactly what is it anyway? What's so good about doing it? Can you think of anything specially interesting that has happened?

You ought to be able to write about a page, and probably more. Try to write in paragraphs, if you can.

Check.
Have it marked.

16 *Imagine!*

Imagine what would happen if . . . If you don't use your imagination, sooner or later you won't be able to imagine anything at all. You need to exercise your imagination, just as much as you need to exercise your muscles, or your brain.

1 Suppose you were kidnapped. Now why should anyone want to kidnap *you*? – that's the first thing. Did they think your parents were rich, and so they could get a lot of money if they sent you back? Did they make a mistake and think you were somebody else? Or what?

Imagine that you have been kidnapped. How did it happen, where were you taken, and why were you taken anyway? Then what happened? What did you do about it, like trying to get away? If so, how? And then what?

Start thinking. Then give it a title:

KIDNAPPED

and **write a story** about it.

Remember – speech marks if anyone says anything. Try to write in paragraphs.

When the story has come to an end –
Check everything.
Have it marked.

2 One evening you happen to look out of the window. Or perhaps you've just gone outside for something. Then just outside where you live you see a thing like a football, only it's glowing green. While you look at it, there's a humming noise, then what look like metal rods start to come out towards you.

What happens next?

Give it a title:

The Yarnos have Landed

Then get on with it!

Check.
Have it marked.

17 *Using facts*

To make a *survey* means to gather some facts, then see what can be discovered from them.

1 Make a survey of pocket money. Everyone in the class writes on a piece of paper how much pocket money is received each week. No name is put on the paper, but just whether you are a boy or a girl. (Why could that information be useful?)

Then the teacher collects the papers and writes each amount on the blackboard, separately for boys and girls.

2 Find out how many boys have to work round the house to get pocket money. Do the same for the girls. Find if any boys do a job for somebody else for which they get paid. Then do the same for the girls. These numbers also go on the blackboard.

3 How many *have* to save some of their money? How many save without being made to? Put these numbers on the board.

4 Now add up all the boys' money. Divide that money by the number of boys in the class, and this gives the *average* pocket money for the boys. Then do the same to find the average pocket money received by the girls. (You can work this out with the teacher on the blackboard.)

5 **Copy** the facts from the blackboard. Then **answer** *in sentences*:

(**a**) What is the biggest amount of pocket money for a boy?
(**b**) What is the biggest amount for a girl?
(**c**) What are the smallest amounts for a boy and a girl? (If the answer is *none*, how many don't get any money at all?)
(**d**) Is there any difference between the *average* pocket money for boys and the *average* for girls? If there is a difference, can you think of any reason why?
(**e**) If any of the class do work round the house, do more girls have to, or more boys, or is it about the same?
(**f**) How many save some of their money?
(**g**) Is your own pocket money less or more than the average (depending on whether you're a boy or a girl), and by how much?
(**h**) Did anything surprise you about the results? Or did it all come out more or less as you expected that it would?

6 So what about *your* pocket money? You must have some money sometime. So how much do you get, and who gives it to you? Do you have to earn it, or is it given to you anyway – or just when you need some?

What do you spend it on? Do you manage to save any? If you had more, what would you do with it? Do you think you *need* more? Or – even – do you think you get too much?

Write about your pocket money. I've suggested how it can be in two paragraphs, if you've noticed.

Check.
Have it marked.

7 If this survey turned out to be interesting – or useful, because if your money is less than the average you might be able to persuade somebody to give you more! – you could do a different survey sometime, like on favourite foods, or parents' jobs – or anything.

18 *Holiday postcards*

On a picture postcard there is not much writing space, just half of one side, so you have to shorten everything which you want to say. That means you don't need to write in sentences, nor put your holiday address. It also means that you have to write neatly so that you can get everything in. That applies as well to the address of the person you're sending it to.

The address goes on the right-hand side and the message on the left-hand side of the postcard. It is best to write the name and address first, before putting anything else. Why?

To start the message, put the *day*. Don't begin with *Dear . . .*, because there's not enough room. Then write the message.

Suppose this is what you wanted to say:

The journey was slow, because there was a lot of traffic on the road, so we didn't arrive here till about six o'clock. The weather is very hot, and we've spent most of today on the beach and in the sea. It's a good job the weather is good, though, because there's not much to do in this place if it rains. Where we are staying is very clean and friendly, but I don't think much of the food. When we come back home, I'll come round and tell you about the holiday. After all, it's only the second day yet, so it might get better, or it might get worse.

You'd never fit it in! So it must be cut down. Something like this:

Slow journey, arrived 6 p.m. Weather hot, spending most time on beach and in sea. Not much else here. Hotel all right, but food not much good. See you when I come back.

Then you put your name at the end – no *Yours sincerely* or anything like that – there isn't room.

Look again at the example. Notice what sort of words are missed out, and what information you have to cut right out.

1 Draw a space, 14 cm by about 9 cm. Find the centre (at 7 cm from either end) and draw a line down. Like this:

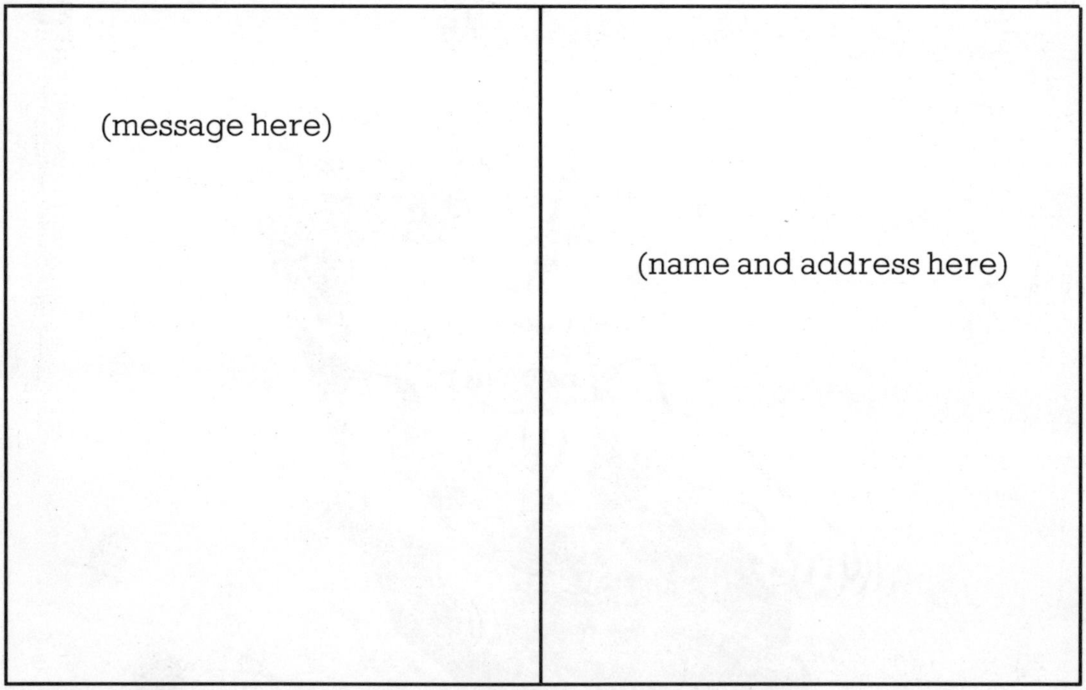

2 Write a friend's name and address in the space on the right. (Don't forget, leave enough space for the stamp, and put the main town in capital letters.)

3 You're on holiday at the seaside. You went by coach, and you weren't sick on the way. Where you are staying is very good, with television, a games room, good food – the lot. The town has got everything, a big sandy beach, a fairground, amusement arcade, lots of things to do. Everywhere is nice and clean, and the hotel is just across the road from the beach and only a few minutes away from everything else. The only trouble is, it's pouring down with rain and has been ever since you arrived.

Write your message in the space on the left side of the postcard.

Check. Message clear? It fitted the space? No mistakes in the address? If so, **have it marked**.

19 *General knowledge*

You need to know what's going on in the world. Test yourself against this quiz. One word will often be a long enough answer, and spelling doesn't count.

Mark your own as the teacher gives the answers. If there's time left, the teacher might make up a few more questions.

1 What do you call a man who looks after sheep?
2 What do you call a field where apple or pear trees grow?
3 Give one word meaning a hundred years.
4 How long is a decade?
5 What continent is Australia in?
6 Give the motto of the Scouts and Guides.
7 Name the capital city of Scotland.
8 Who is the Prime Minister of Great Britain?
9 What is butter made from?
10 What do you call a place for keeping a car?
11 What do you call a boat which goes under water?
12 Name the longest river in Britain.
13 How many legs has a tripod?
14 What do you call an instrument for measuring time?
15 What do you call the low ground between two hills?
16 What name is given to a bigger boy or girl who frightens smaller ones?
17 What name is given to a watering place in a desert?
18 What special name is given to a religious song?
19 What is odd about a Manx cat?
20 On a colour TV, what three colours make up all the others?
21 What do you call a three-sided figure?
22 Who is the President of the USA?
23 In Scotland there are many *lochs*. What is a loch?
24 If you walk in Indian file, what does it mean?
25 What do you call the middle part of an apple?

20 *Spelling*

In the alphabet, the *vowels* are **a**, **e**, **i**, **o** and **u**. These are the sounds you make with your mouth open. But a vowel can be long or short: an **e** can be a long sound, like in *steel*, or short like in *men*; an **a** can be long, as in *make*, or short as in *hat*.

Find examples of long and short **i**, **o** and **u**.

1 *stoped* or *stopped* – which is the right spelling? How do you know?

Look at the word *stop*. It has a short **o** sound. If you want to spell *stop(-ed)* or *stop(-ing)*, *because it's a short vowel sound* you double the letter after the vowel. So the words are spelt *sto**pp**ed* and *sto**pp**ing*.

If it's a long vowel sound, do not double the letter. **Spell** these: read(-ing), thin(-er), break(-able), rob(-ery), step(-ing).

2 Look at the words *label* and *conceal*.

You spell *labe**ll**ed* and *labe**ll**ing*, but *concea**l**ed* and *concea**l**ing*. Why the difference?

It's because there is a short vowel in front of the **l** in label. So – *short vowel sound, double the letter **l***.

How many vowels are there in front of the **l** in *conceal*?

So – if there's more than one vowel, leave the **l** alone. **Spell** these: feel(-ing), pedal(-ing), reveal(-ing), marvel(-ous), pencil(-ed).

3 Words ending in **r** or **t** have special rules, depending on the number of *syllables* in the word.

A syllable is a complete sound in a word. *And* has only one syllable, but *reading* has two syllables – *read* and *ing*. Motoring has three syllables – *mo-tor-ing*.

In English, we stress part of a word if there is more than one syllable. Like if you *regret* something (you're sorry about something), do you say reGRET, or do you say REgret? Say it aloud and you'll find you say reGRET.

If a word ends in **r** or **t**, and it's got more than one syllable, if you put some stress on the *first* syllable, *don't double the last letter*.

But if you stress the *last* syllable, *follow the rule* about short vowel sounds and long vowel sounds.

This looks difficult, but it isn't. How do you spell defeat(-ed)?

Work it out:

(**a**) Do you say DEfeat, or deFEAT? It's the second way.
(**b**) How many vowels in front of the last **t**? – Two.
(**c**) Follow the rule – leave the **t** alone. So the word is spelt *defea**t**ed*.

How do you spell refer(-ing)?

(**a**) REfer, or reFER? It's reFER.
(**b**) How many vowels before the last **r**? There's one.
(**c**) So follow the rule – single vowel, double the letter **r**. The word is spelt *refe**rr**ing*.

4 **Spell** these words:
repair(-ed), alter(-ing), suffer(-ing), differ(-ence), occur(-ed).

5 Now **Spell** these:
await(-ed), fidget(-ing), outwit(-ed), commit(-ed), benefit(-ed).
Beware of the last word. If you spell it right, it looks wrong, but it isn't!

Check. You could have found the last ten words tricky. If you need to, look at the instructions again before you **have it marked**. 15 or more right is *very* good.

The next time you wonder whether to double a letter or not, if you can't remember find these pages and look up the rules again.

6 It's a good idea if about every half-term the teacher gives a spelling test from mistakes found in your books. It doesn't take long to start getting most of them right. (Notice – I used two **t**'s in *getting* – of course.)

21 *Codes*

When two foreign spies were arrested in London, the only reason they were known to be spies was because they had tiny code books on them – just as big as postage stamps.

A message in code will keep the message secret for a while, but it must be spelt right or nobody would know what the message was.

First you need the alphabet, because it's easier if it is in front of you.

1 Write out the alphabet, in capital letters. If you need to use more than one line, leave a gap between the two lines.

ABCDEFGHIJKLMNOPQRSTUVWXYZ

2 Now you need a number, such as a telephone number with not more than about seven digits in it. Perhaps use the school telephone number, or part of it.

Look at this message:

SEE YOU LATER TONIGHT

I'm going to use the telephone number 2373214.

You write the message like this:

SEE YOU LATER TONIGHT

237 321 42373 2142373

– that is, you repeat the number underneath the message until the message runs out.

Then you move each letter of your message forward in the alphabet as many times as each number says. **S** (+ 2) becomes **U**. **E** (+ 3) becomes **H**. **E** (+ 7) becomes **L**.

So SEE is written in code as UHL . . . and so on.

To work it back, anyone with the alphabet in front of them writes under the message the same numbers as you were using, but counts *backwards* in the alphabet instead of forward.

Got the idea?

The only thing is, whoever receives your message *must* know the code number you are using. If they don't the code is very difficult to break, except by a real expert.

3 Think up a short message which makes sense. You are going to send it to someone else in the same class, but *not* anyone sitting near you. Perhaps this time the whole class should use the same code number.

Print out your message, and send it. (**Check** – spelt right? No mistakes in the numbers?)

4 When anyone has worked out a message, it goes back to its sender. If anyone can't work it out, either that person didn't understand how to do it, or you didn't work it out right in the first place.

5 Now you know how to do it, you can send a message to any friend, in secret, as long as your friend knows the code number first. Nobody else will be able to break the code at all, unless they suddenly think of what the code number could be. Very useful!

The Chinese use a different form of writing from ours: each sign stands for a whole idea, not just one letter. Can you try inventing a sign for 'the house under the tree'?

22 *Words*

The more words you know, the more you can think, because usually you think in words.

1 Reading – anything – helps you to be able to use more words, and so to think better. In the meantime, try these. After each word are three possible meanings. Only one meaning is right.
Write each word, and after it **A**, **B** or **C** depending on which meaning you think is the right one. If you don't know, either guess sensibly or use a dictionary.

(a) **Adorn** If you adorn yourself with rings and things, do you
A decorate yourself
B worship yourself
C make yourself perfect
(If you think it means 'to worship yourself', you just put a letter **B** after the word.)

(b) **Tiff** Have you ever had a tiff with anybody? If so, was it
A a snack
B a quarrel
C a joke

(c) **Extinct** You can't be this, because it means
A vanished
B all fuzzy
C separate from everything else

(d) **Obese** If somebody's obese, he or she is
A fat
B kind
C noisy

(e) **Aerial** You've got one on your television. But does it mean
A long and thin
B made of metal
C in the air

(f) **Alms** (It sounds like arms.) You might know of some alms houses, where old people live.
A prayer
B to do with those who can't walk
C charity

(g) **Pilfer** If you pilfer, you
A annoy
B add up
C steal

(h) **Arcade** Like an amusement arcade. But an arcade is really
A a parade
B a theatre
C covered passageway

(i) **Suet** Like in a suet pudding. It's
A a sort of gravy
B animal fat
C flour

(j) **Fleecy** Like fleecy boots
A soft and light
B quick
C heavy

(k) **Safari** Like a safari park, or you might go on safari. So it's
A a wasteland
B a journey
C a strong wind

(l) **Solvent** They use it in glue.
A putty
B a fastener
C makes things dissolve

(m) **Corrode** If metal corrodes, it
A wears through
B gets clean
C turns brown

(n) **Wean** Babies are weaned, like all young animals. They
A get born
B stop sucking milk
C grow bigger

(o) **Transfix** If somebody's transfixed, he's
A been propped up
B got a spike through him
C fallen asleep

(p) **Peruse** Have you ever perused a book? If so, you've
A gone through it quickly
B gone through it carefully
C ignored it

(q) **Spacious** If a room or a house is spacious, it is
A small
B large
C cramped

(r) **Canister** You might have a canister of spray paint. So it's
A something that works like a gun
B a shelter
C a container

(s) **Strew** Somebody strewed your things about
A to destroy
B to scatter
C to search for

(t) **Veer** If the wind veers, does it
A move faster
B move slower
C turn round

Check. Anything you want to change? Then do it neatly.
Have it marked. Find out who's got most right in the class.

2 It's no good just knowing words, if you don't use them. The teacher will pick out some of these words for you to *use* in a sentence, in such a way it is clear that you know what each word means.

For instance, if the word *wean* is chosen, you can use *wean*, or *weaned*, or *weaning*, as long as your sentence using that word shows that you understand its meaning.

When you've finished -
Check. Capital letters to start? Full stops or question marks to end? Can be read easily?
If so, **have it marked**.

23 *Head teacher*

If you were the Head Teacher of your school, what changes would you make?

You cannot: sack any teachers (hard luck!); change the main school holiday dates; knock down part of the school or have something new built (but you can ask for something like that to be done); or change the school hours very much – if you start later, you have to finish later, for example.

You can: make everyone wear a uniform, or say there isn't going to be a uniform; decide what lessons classes are to have, and how long each lesson is to last; which teachers are to teach which classes; what punishments there are going to be, and what you might punish for.

Discuss anything else you can think of, about what a Head Teacher can do and can't do.

Now you are the Head Teacher. What are you going to do about it? Are there any changes you are going to make – and why? Is there anything you want altered, or stopped altogether – and why?

Think first. Then give it a title:

If I Were the Head Teacher

Try to put it into paragraphs. Ask for any spellings.

When you've written all you can think of, with reasons –

Check.
Have it marked.

24 *This year at school*

This is a chance to say what you really think, but you have to go about it the right way. Some people can't tell the difference between being blunt and being rude. (Well, what is the difference?)

Also you should use the right words. 'It's a load of rubbish,' you might think. Sorry – that doesn't mean anything. And if you are going to say that something is not right, you'd better be able to think of something better to put in its place. If there is something wrong – exactly what, and how would you put it right or do something different to improve it? Have you any ideas about something which isn't wrong, but which doesn't happen at your school and you think it should?

This last bit of the book could fit either the beginning or the end of a school year, or you could even change the title to *Last Year At School* instead. But you've got the chance to say what you think, how you really feel, for once . . .

But – it's to be in proper words, carefully thought out. What's good about the year? What's not so good? What did you like and what didn't you like at all? How did it compare with the year before, if you can remember?

It's up to you. **Check** it through when you've finished, of course.
Then **have it marked** in the usual way.

Index for the Teacher

This grid shows the main skills practised in each topic. Further cross-references are possible in that most topics end with written work, all involve reading, and each one should ultimately be functional in purpose.

		Writing	*Writing Skills*	*Oral*	*Imaginative*	*Functional*	*Page*
1	**Making sense**	●	●				6
2	**Talking**			●			8
3	**How to use it**	●					10
4	**Atlas**					●	12
5	**Clothes**	●			●		13
6	**Letters**		●				14
7	**Acting**			●			16
8	**Friends**	●					19
9	**Your family**	●				●	20
10	**Handwriting**		●				22
11	**Speech marks**		●				24
12	**How it feels**				●		26
13	**Cars**					●	28
14	**Joining up sentences**		●				30
15	**Out of school**	●					31
16	**Imagine!**				●		32
17	**Using facts**					●	34
18	**Holiday postcards**		●				36
19	**General knowledge**					●	38
20	**Spelling**		●				40
21	**Codes**					●	42
22	**Words**		●				44
23	**Head Teacher**				●		46
24	**This year at school**	●					47